# A Lent Companion

*An anthology of reflections and prayers for those in ministry*

Compiled by Arthur Howells
With a foreword by Rowan Williams

A Redemptorist Publication

Published by **Redemptorist Publications**

Copyright © 2005 Redemptorist Publications

Cover design: Arcus Design
Design: Peena Lad

First Edition January 2005

ISBN 0 85231 297 0

Printed by Cambridge University Press

**Redemptorist**
PUBLICATIONS

Alphonsus House Chawton Hampshire GU34 3HQ
Telephone 01420 88222      Fax 01420 88805
rp@ShineOnline.net          www.ShineOnline.net

*Arthur Howells* is a retired Anglican priest who has served all his ministry in the Church in Wales. He is married to Margaret, and they have two sons and four grandchildren. Formerly Canon Residentiary and Chancellor of Brecon Cathedral, he was Canon Missioner of the Diocese of Swansea and Brecon for ten years prior to his last appointment as Vicar of St James', Swansea. He assists in local parishes and conducts Retreats and Quiet Days. He was recently awarded an MA in Celtic Christianity by the University of Wales, Lampeter.

## Foreword

In one of the pieces in this fine anthology, Canon Howells quotes Archbishop Michael Ramsey as telling us to "make friends with the greatest writers, in biblical exposition, in Christian doctrine, in the classics of Christian spirituality". This is a book which is meant to help us make friends – not only with the great expositors of our age, but with some more modest fellow-travellers too, who can at least give words to the challenges we face. But here you will find Henri Nouwen and Austin Farrer, Evelyn Underhill and Thomas Merton, Dietrich Bonhoeffer and Anthony Bloom – the undoubted, definitive voices of modern faith, whose witness makes us see how it is possible after all to be a thinking Christian in our days without losing the heart of the tradition.

It has always been a great strength in Arthur Howells' long and creative priestly ministry that he has been deeply grounded in this tradition and continuously, generously open. We are privileged to be allowed to read over his shoulder, as it were, the texts that have nourished that ministry. Thanks to this book, they will nourish many more in the same service of God and God's people. These are the tools for a faith and witness utterly contemporary, utterly honest about a world of terrors and sufferings and doubts, yet also firm in loyalty to the faith received. They testify to the abiding relevance of Christ incarnate and his Holy Spirit, and to the end of all our journeying which is the Father's heart.

Rowan Williams, Archbishop of Canterbury.

## Introduction

This anthology consists of extracts and prayers drawn from a variety of sources. Over the years, especially while on retreat or sharing reflections at a Quiet Day, I have picked up a book or read an article which has really spoken to me. I selected some of these in the hope that what I have found helpful may speak to others too, and may provide that encouragement or challenge which we all need from time to time as we continue our journey through this life.

The difficulty with such a selection is to know what to leave out! While my choice for each day has been somewhat haphazard, I have attempted to capture something of the atmosphere of this wonderful season of Lent, leading us, as it does, to Passiontide and Easter where the readings and accompanying prayers have been chosen more carefully for their appropriateness.

My hope and prayer is that this small *Lent Companion* will be used as yet another resource to help us along our pilgrim journey as we share with the crucified and risen Lord something of his journey.

I am most grateful to Marguerite Hutchinson, Commissioning Editor of Redemptorist Publications, for her help and encouragement.

Arthur Howells

# Ash Wednesday: *Reality*

Each Lent of our life should be more real in its approach to God than the last. Reality in the spiritual life means becoming more and more interior in one's religion. All exterior things have their value in as much as they are expressions of an interior reality, but as life goes on it is less and less the outward, and more and more the inward, that has real meaning for the soul. In the childhood of the soul, feelings and sentimental consciousness and outward things like the ritual of the Church, will have their very real place in the soul's development. But as the spiritual sense is developed, less and less will the things of sight and sense and sound have value, and more and more will the things of the spirit and silence and the choice of the will be important.

To some, perhaps, this Lent may be a (new) beginning … To others it may be that Lent is to be the consecration of pain and a strengthening of the will. To all it should be a coming to reality. A definition of reality might be "that of which the outward expression has an inward equivalent", and it is of course the inward equivalent that alone gives outward expression its value. The point for all of us is to try to make our religion more and more real, and, as outward things mean less and less to us, to be quite sure that inward things mean more, that as the attraction fades away from what is outward and what is sensible so it deepens in what is interior and what is of the will.

*Meditations for Every Day:* Fr Andrew

*Spirit of integrity,*
*You drive us into the desert*
*To search out our truth.*
*Give us charity to know what is right,*
*And courage to reject what is strategic;*
*That we may abandon the false innocence*
*Of failing to choose at all,*
*But may follow the purposes of Jesus.*

All Desires Known: *Janet Morley*

# Thursday: *The Island of Prayer*

To get to Holy Island, off the coast of Northumberland, you have to wait for low tide, in order to cross the sands by means of the causeway, which is accessible for only a few hours between the tides. A causeway is revered as an especially sacred place in the Celtic mind and heart. It is a place of transition, a means of passing from where you are to where you desire to be. In this sense you might call a causeway a channel of grace. But it is also a powerful parable of prayer.

Use your imagination to picture the mainland, the causeway, and the island. Let the tide ebb, and then walk quietly across, as if you were walking into the sacred space of silence and prayer. Is there anything specific, any issue in your life that you are carrying with you today from the mainland to the island? If so, simply let it be there, without any deliberate effort to resolve it. Allow the stillness of the holy place to receive you, welcome you, enfold you. And as you sink into the stillness, allow the tide to come in and encircle you in your island-space. Slowly the causeway disappears, submerged in the rising tides. You are alone with God on the island of your prayer.

Eventually the tide turns. Your time of prayer is over. The water recedes. The causeway begins to reappear. It is time for the return journey, back to the mainland. Perhaps you are eager to return, relieved that the time of prayer has passed, if it has been difficult or dry. Perhaps you are reluctant to return, wishing your island time could last for ever. Either way the mainland beckons you. It is time to *re-connect* to the place of your lived life.

Make friends with your causeway. Gradually let yourself become familiar with the feeling of moving backwards and forwards between the "island" of your prayer and the "mainland" of your daily life. Begin to notice the rhythm of your own "tides", and the natural interactions between "high tide", when you are alone with God on the island, and "low tide", when you are wholly engaged with the demands and strains of life in your personal circumstances. Notice, and perhaps make a written note of, any issues you are carrying from the mainland to the island, and any gifts you are taking back from the island to the mainland. Are these gifts for yourself, do you think, or for other people as well? Welcome this "trade route" in your heart, and let it become fruitful. Become more aware of what you are hoping for from it, and how these hopes are being fulfilled.

*Taste and See:* Margaret Silf

*Fill us, we pray, Lord,*
*With your light and life*
*That we may show forth your wondrous glory.*
*Grant that your love may so fill our lives*
*That we may count nothing too small to do for you,*
*Nothing too much to give*
*And nothing too hard to bear.*

# Friday: *Preaching*

aul urged Timothy to be "a workman who had no
need to be ashamed, rightly handling the word of
truth". John Stott helpfully comments on this verse:

> The verb *orthotomounta* [rightly handling] means
> literally, "cutting straight". It was employed of road-
> making and is, for instance, used in the LXX of
> Proverbs 3:6: "He will make straight (AV, direct) your
> paths." Our exposition of the Scripture is to be so
> simple and direct, so easily intelligible, that it
> resembles a straight road. It is easy to follow it. It is like
> Isaiah's highway of the redeemed: even "fools shall not
> err therein". Such straight cutting of the Word of God
> is not easy. It requires much study ... not only of God's
> Word but of man's nature and of the world in which he
> lives. The expository preacher is a bridge builder,
> seeking to span the gulf between the Word of God and
> mind of man. He must do his utmost to interpret the
> Scripture so accurately and plainly, and to apply it so
> forcefully, that the truth crosses the bridge.

The poverty of preaching in much of today's church is
probably due to the poverty of Bible study. If the preacher
is to dispense God's word effectively week after week, year
after year, and still remain fresh and relevant, there will be
no substitute for the dogged discipline of daily study. He
must learn to grasp the broad sweep of scriptural truth as
well as examining carefully the detailed text. He must ask
himself: "What is the meaning of this word or phrase?

What is its relevance and application to my life, and to needs of this particular part of the body of Christ? How can it be explained and illustrated?"

We need to be soaked in the Scriptures. We must "let the word of Christ dwell in us richly in all wisdom". We shall need modern translations and commentaries, the original text, a lexicon, a concordance and a Bible dictionary. Most of all we need the illumination of the Holy Spirit. Our aim is not to produce a commentary on the passage in question, but to discover and deliver God's message for the occasion. With some confidence we should be able to stand up and say, as it were, "Thus says the Lord".

*I Believe in the Church:* David Watson

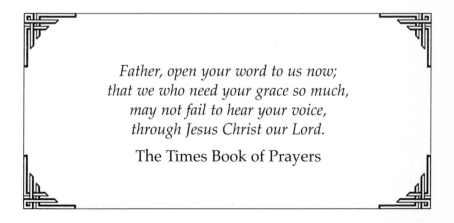

*Father, open your word to us now;*
*that we who need your grace so much,*
*may not fail to hear your voice,*
*through Jesus Christ our Lord.*

The Times Book of Prayers

# Saturday: *A Sign of Sanctity?*

It is in your prayer that you serve your people best, being as Archbishop Michael Ramsey put it "before God with the people in your heart – being with Him for them and with them for Him". Such is the nature of our priestly service. Hildegard of Bingen reminds us of that holiness of life to which we are called – the priest in particular – the priest as a sign of sanctity. She was not a particularly easy person to live with, but then whoever is? At times downright obstinate and objectionable yet even out of these "weaknesses" God's amazing grace triumphs to bring forth her greatest strengths...

The priest as a sign of sanctity, of holiness, speaks to us of the wholeness and wholesomeness of our lives, that they are as the Ordinal puts it "framed and fashioned according to the Doctrine of Christ"; that there should be a consonance between the public and the private, above all that we should be ourselves, our own God-given character and characteristics fulfilled in His service.

Hildegard, as with so many of the saints, is an encouragement to us that we should not give up on ourselves, for God never does. Rather, in those moments of our greatest lostness and God-forsakenness he is there bearing with us, holding, giving, loving. The signs of our sanctity are not to be found in the sanctuary, rather they will be evidenced in the way in which we treat one another and not least where there are sharp differences of view, strong and acute feelings on one side or the other on a particular issue or subject, controversial matters which constantly threaten to divide and yet where we are all called to strive fervently for that unity of the spirit in the bond of peace. For what hope is there for so many out there who are seeking, searching, surfing, if the Church is so wholly consumed with its own internal agendas? It is St Hildegard who points the way when she writes:

> People retain a glimmering of their knowledge of God. They should allow God to return to the centre of their lives, recognising that they owe their very existence to no one else save God alone, who is the creator of all.

So the question for us is how is it possible to allow God to return to the centre of people's lives, beginning of course with ourselves and our churches? Does the worship, the prayer, the life of our Church and congregation in all its aspects enable people to apprehend something of the beauty, the splendour, the glory, the love of God, or is it all but some pale reflection of our own supposedly well-devised policies and strategies?

*Signs of Hope:* David Hope

*O God, the Holy Spirit*
*You have come to us*
*You are with us.*
*You have come as the wind – Cleanse us*
*You have come as the fire – Consume us*
*You have come as the dew – Refresh us*
*Convict, convert and consecrate many hearts and lives*
*to our great good and your greater glory*
*through Jesus Christ our Lord.*

15

# Lent 1: *Being the Beloved*

Jesus shows us the way of compassion, not only by what he says, but also by how he lives. Jesus speaks and lives as the Beloved Son of God. One of the most central events of Jesus' life is related by Matthew: "When Jesus had been baptized he at once came up from the water, and suddenly, the heavens opened and he saw the Spirit of God descending like a dove and coming down on him. And suddenly there was a voice from heaven, 'This is my Son, the Beloved: my favour rests on him.'"

The event reveals the true identity of Jesus. Jesus is the Beloved Son of God. This spiritual truth will guide all his thoughts, words, and actions. It is the rock on which his compassionate ministry will be built. This becomes very obvious when we are told that the same Spirit who descended on him when he came up from the water, also led him into the desert to be tempted. There the "Tempter" said to him: "Do something useful, like turning stones into bread. Do something sensational, like throwing yourself down from a high tower. Do something that brings you power, like paying me homage." These three temptations were three ways to seduce Jesus into becoming a competitor for love. The world of the "Tempter" is precisely that world in which people compete for love through doing useful, sensational, and powerful things and so winning medals that gain them affection and admiration.

Jesus, however, is very clear in his response: "I don't have to prove that I am worthy of love. I am the Beloved of God, the One on whom God's favour rests." It was that victory over the "Tempter" that set Jesus free to choose for the compassionate life.

*Here and Now:* Henri Nouwen

*Lord God,*
*guide us on our Lenten journey,*
*that we may recognise and resist all temptation*
*to put self-interest before your truth.*
*For you are the way*
*and there is no other approach to your Kingdom.*
*We make this prayer in Jesus' name.*

With Christ in the Wilderness:
*Derek Worlock and David Sheppard*

# Monday after Lent 1: *The Listening God*

Y ou need to pray in stillness and in quietude. People say they go out to look at the stars on the hillside. Jesus says don't do it: go into the closet, shut the door. I find I have to be in darkness really to pray. In stillness and in quietude I focus on Jesus. I don't say anything. Mother Teresa was once asked: "When you pray, what do you say to God?" She said: "I don't say anything. I listen." So the interviewer said: "Alright. What does God say to you?" She said: "God doesn't say anything. God listens." And then she added: "If you can't understand that, I can't explain it to you."

The deepest kind of prayers are not when we tell God the things God already knows. It's when we become still, focused, centred down, in quietude. I have to say the name "Jesus" over and over again to drive away the hundred and one things that are waiting to be done that absorb my consciousness. And in the stillness, I allow Jesus to invade me, to possess me, the same Jesus who died on the cross, the same Jesus who was resurrected. Because the Kingdom of God starts that way. It starts with a people who in stillness and in quietude surrender to a presence, and become new people.

When the Spirit of Christ invades you, you are capable of finding Jesus in people that you meet – especially in the poor and the oppressed. The Kingdom of God: a society in which people are transformed, in order that through them God might eliminate hunger, oppression, disease, transform the world that is into the Kingdom of God.

*A Sermon at Greenbelt:* Tony Campolo

*O God,*
*who art the light of the minds that know thee,*
*the life of the souls that love thee,*
*and the strength of the hearts that serve thee;*
*help us so to know thee that we may truly love thee;*
*so to love thee that we may fully serve thee,*
*whom to serve is perfect freedom;*
*through Jesus Christ our Lord.*

Gelasian Sacramentary

# Tuesday after Lent 1: *The Sound of Silence*

What can help people to find answers to their own mystery and the mystery of him in whose image they are created, is *silence, solitude – in a word, the desert.* We need these things today more than the hermits of old.

If we are to witness to Christ in today's marketplaces, where there are constant demands on our own person, we need silence. If we are to be always available, not only physically, but by empathy, sympathy, friendship, understanding and boundless *caritas*, we need silence. To be able to give joyous, unflagging hospitality, not only of house and food, but of mind, heart, body and soul, we need silence.

True silence is the search of man for God.

True silence is the suspension bridge that a soul in love with God builds to cross the dark, frightening gullies of its own mind, the strange chasms of temptation, the depthless precipices of its own fears that impede its way to God.

True silence is the speech of lovers. For only love knows its beauty, completeness, and utter joy. True silence is a garden enclosed, where alone the soul can meet its God. It is a sealed fountain that he alone can unseal to slacken the soul's infinite thirst for him.

This silence is not the exclusive prerogative of monasteries or convents. This simple, prayerful silence is everybody's silence – or if it isn't, it should be. It belongs to every Christian who loves God, to every Jew who has heard in his heart the echoes of God's voice in the prophets, to everyone whose soul has risen in search of truth, in search of God. For where there is noise – inward noise and confusion – there God is not!

*Poustinia:* Catherine de Hueck Doherty

*You, Lord, are in this place*
*Your presence fills it*
*Your presence is Peace.*

*You, Lord, are in my heart*
*Your presence fills it*
*Your presence is Peace.*

*You, Lord, are in my mind*
*Your presence fills it*
*Your presence is Peace.*

*You, Lord, are in my life*
*Your presence fills it*
*Your presence is Peace.*

*Help us, O Lord, to know that we dwell in you*
*And you dwell in us this day and evermore.*

The Open Gate: *David Adam*

# Wednesday after Lent 1: *Prayer is Knowing God*

At the beginning of a relationship there's often a period of infatuation; all you want to do is to spend time with the other person. As it is with prayer: when you begin to pray, all you want is to spend time with God, so enjoyable is it. But the relationship needs to move beyond that superficial level to something deeper. Like any friendship, it needs to grow and be open to change. And so prayer changes throughout your life; sometimes it will come naturally, almost easily, and feel rich and deep; at other times, prayer will be exceedingly difficult, almost a chore, and yield precious little in the way of "result". But the important thing is – again, as in any friendship – to keep at it, and, ultimately, to come to know and love the other person deeply. As the Jesuit theologian Karl Rahner wrote, the important thing is not knowing *about* God, it is knowing God.

Part of prayer is also the basic trust that for those who seek God sincerely, God will eventually come. As one Islamic saying has it, for every step you take towards God, God takes two steps towards you; and if you come to God walking, God comes to you running.

*In Good Company: The Fast Track from the Corporate World to Poverty, Chastity and Obedience:* James Martin SJ

*Lord Jesus,*
*save us from over-confidence or despair.*
*It is only because you are our Lord*
*that we may presume to show the way to others.*
*Help us lest we stumble*
*over our own self-importance;*
*and when we trip over our own feet,*
*give us the humble faith to get up and go on.*
*Through the same Christ our Lord.*

# Thursday after Lent 1: *Who am I?*

Who am I? They often tell me
I would step from my cell's confinement
calmly, cheerfully, firmly,
like a squire from his country house.

Who am I? They often tell me
I would talk to my warders
freely and friendly and clearly,
as though it were mine to command.

Who am I? They also tell me
I would bear days of misfortune
equably, smilingly, proudly,
like one accustomed to win.

Am I then really all that which other men tell of?
Or am I only what I know of myself,
restless and longing and sick, like a bird in a cage,
struggling for breath, as though hands were
compressing my throat,
yearning for colours, for flowers,
for the voices of birds,

thirsting for words of kindness, for neighbourliness,
trembling with anger at despotisms and
petty humiliation,
tossing in expectation of great events,
powerlessly trembling for friends at
infinite distance,
weary and empty at praying, at thinking, at making,
faint, and ready to say farewell to it all?

Who am I? This or the other?
Am I one person today, and tomorrow another?
Am I both at once? A hypocrite before others,
and before myself a contemptibly
woebegone weakling?
Or is something within me still like a beaten army,
fleeing in disorder from victory already achieved?

Who am I? They mock me, these lonely
questions of mine.
Whoever I am, thou knowest, O God, I am thine.

*Letters and Papers from Prison:* Dietrich Bonhoeffer

# Friday after Lent 1: *The Priest's Life of Prayer*

The priest's life of prayer, his communion with God, is not only his primary obligation to the Church; it is also the only condition under which the work of the Christian ministry can be properly done. He is called, as the Book of Wisdom says, to be a "friend of God, and a prophet"; and will only be a good prophet in so far as he is really a friend of God. For his business is to lead men out towards eternity; and how can he do this unless it is a country in which he is at home? He is required to represent the peace of God in a troubled society; but that is impossible if he has not the habit of resorting to those deeps of the spirit where His Presence dwells.

A consecrated life, which must be the goal of the priest's interior prayer, is a life which, having been offered without reserve, is transformed by God, and made what it ought to be: a sacrament of His life and love, a means whereby that life and love are communicated to other souls. It is as sharing in some faint degree in the Lord's High Priestly action, bringing the needs of the world to the altar of God; and going forth from the altar of God, bringing bread and wine to the needs of the world, that the Christian priest's life of prayer must be lived.

And this rich life of prayer, again and again, bringing him close to things infinite and eternal, yet never separating him from the natural life, he shall lift up to God, offer in its wholeness, for the manifold needs of people.

Here is the mould into which he can pour all his thirst for God, all his self-giving to God, all his love and concern for souls.

*A Priests' Retreat:* Evelyn Underhill

*Father, be merciful to us, who are poor instruments of your peace. Enlighten our minds, increase our faith, give us the joy of knowing that we work for you, and especially give us a share of your love for humanity. We make our prayer through your Son, Jesus Christ our Lord.*

# Saturday after Lent 1: *The Heart of the Priest*

The only priesthood is that of Christ, and it is entrusted into our hands ... Can we ever belittle the heavy responsibility that has been laid on our shoulders?

We carry a burden, but we recognise that the burden of Christ is sweet and his yoke light. He gives the help we need, so there is never any reason for us to fear, to draw back or to be discouraged. Christ enables us all the time to respond to his call, as fresh and vivid today and as compelling, as it was on the day of our Ordination.

Have I the heart of a priest? Is my heart in my priesthood? Or has my treasure become something other than my priesthood? Do I sense still a certain thrill as I go to the altar to celebrate Mass, or is it a bit different now? Do I long to speak to the people of the good news of the Gospel, or has it become dull and uninteresting for me, and so uninteresting when I speak about it? Do I love the sick and the poor? Does my priestly heart still feel for those in distress? Do I feel awe and reverence for the Blessed Sacrament, or has familiarity – or, worse still, doubt – coloured my attitude? Do I still feel a terrible humility and awesome responsibility as I say in the confessional: "I absolve you from your sins..."?

Forgive me, Lord, for my failures and shortcomings, but I know deep down that you use me as you found me, and in spite of myself. That is consoling, but give me, I pray, the heart of a priest, especially a heart that knows the meaning of true love, love of God and love of the people. May I be helped to translate that love into action and into service of others.

*To be a Pilgrim:* Basil Hume

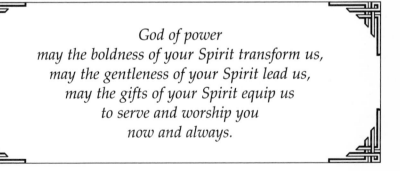

*God of power
may the boldness of your Spirit transform us,
may the gentleness of your Spirit lead us,
may the gifts of your Spirit equip us
to serve and worship you
now and always.*

# Lent 2: *Passing the Light*

S ome time ago I was watching the flicker, almost imperceptible, of a tiny night-light. One of the sisters came up, and having lit her own candle in the dying flame, passed it round to light the candles of the others. And the thought came to me: "Who dares glory in their own good works? It needs but one faint spark to set the world on fire."

We come in touch with burning and shining lights, set high on the candlestick of the Church, and we think we are receiving from them grace and light. But from where do they borrow their fire?

Very possibly from the prayers of some hidden soul whose inward shining is not apparent to human eyes – some soul of unrecognised virtue, and in her own sight of little worth: a dying flame!

What mysteries we shall one day see unveiled! I have often thought that perhaps I owe all the graces with which I am laden to some little soul whom I shall know only in heaven.

*St Thérèse of Lisieux*

*Blessed are you, Lord God, Creator of all.*
*You have called us out of darkness*
*Into your bright light,*
*Into Christ's light.*
*Let his presence guide us this day,*
*That we may share his light*
*And walk before you as children of light,*
*Father, Son, and Holy Spirit.*

The Open Gate: *David Adam*

## Monday after Lent 2: *Dedicated Agents of God's Love*

The soul of a priest, in fact the soul of every religious worker, stands in a special relation towards God and other souls. He is one of the assistant shepherds, not one of the sheep. He has got to stick it out in all weathers; to be always ready, always serving, always eager to feed and save. An unremitting, patient-fostering care, the willing endurance of exhaustion, hardship and risk: all these things may be asked of him.

... You do far more for your congregation, for helping them to understand what prayer really is, and to practise it, for quickening their religious sensitiveness, by your unself-conscious absorption in God during services, than you can hope to do by any amount of sermons... These congregations are probably far too shy to come and tell you what it is that helps them most in the things you do; but there is no doubt at all that your recollectedness, your devotional temper will be one of the things that do help them most.

A priest's life of prayer is, in a peculiar sense, part of the great mystery of the Incarnation. He is meant to be one of the channels by, and through which, the Eternal God, manifested in time, acts within the human world, reaches out, seeks, touches and transforms human souls. His real position in the parish is that of a dedicated agent of Divine Love. The Spirit of Christ, indirectly in His Church, is to act in and through him.

*A Priests' Retreat:* Evelyn Underhill

*Strengthen for service, Lord, the hands that
have taken holy things.
May the ears that have heard your word never
listen to discord.
Keep from carelessness the tongues that
expressed your praise;
Let the eyes which saw the signs of your love
behold the fullness of your Kingdom;
Do not banish from your presence the feet
that stood in your assembly;
Fill with new life the bodies fed by your body.*

Short Prayers for a Long Day: *Giles Harcourt*

# Tuesday after Lent 2: *Walking Sacraments*

… a priest is a living stem, bearing sacraments as its fruits: he gives you the body and blood of Christ: he gives you, if you faithfully confess before him, Christ's own absolution. And that's not all; the man who bears the Sacrament is sacramental himself; he is, one might almost say, himself a walking sacrament. He is the appointed flag for Christ's people to rally round: the centre of unity to which we hold in every place. Just exactly what a priest is, you can best see in the Holy Eucharist. In a great part of the holy action he is, of course, no more than the voice of the congregation. Some of the prayers we say with him, some we let him say for us: it makes little difference. Or again, in receiving the sacrament, the priest is in the same position as any other Christian, receiving the body and blood of Christ. But there is a moment when the priest steps into the place of Christ himself, to do what Christ did, to bless and to break, to present the mysterious sacrifice before God Almighty. It is much the same in absolution. If you have gone and made your confession to the priest, you will understand what I say, when I tell you Christ speaks in him the absolving words.

These moments, certainly, are exceptional in the activity of a priest; exceptional, but still not disconnected with his whole life or character. The man who is as Christ in the Sacrament is not just like anyone else ever: he bears the stamp. He is always, as I said before, a sort of walking sacrament, a token of Christ wherever he is: in him Christ sets up the standard of his kingdom and calls us to the colours.

*A Celebration of Faith:* Austin Farrer

*Dear Lord, help me to keep my eyes on you.*
*You are the incarnation of Divine love,*
*You are the expression of God's infinite compassion,*
*You are the visible manifestation of the Father's holiness.*
*You are beauty, goodness, gentleness,*
*forgiveness and mercy.*
*In all you can be found.*
*Outside of you nothing can be found.*
*Why should I look elsewhere, or go elsewhere?*
*You have the words of eternal life,*
*You are food and drink,*
*You are the Way, the Truth, and the Life.*
*You are the Light that shines in the darkness,*
*The Lamp on the lampstand,*
*The House on the hilltop,*
*You are the perfect Icon of God.*
*In and through you I can see and find my way to the*
*Heavenly Father …*
*To you I want to give all that I am.*
*Let me be generous, not stingy, or hesitant.*
*Let me give you all – all that I think, do, and feel.*
*It is yours, O Lord.*
*Please accept it and make it fully your own.*

Seeds of Hope: *Henri Nouwen*

# Wednesday after Lent 2: *The Priest's Obligation*

Anyone can be a better Christian than a priest, more holy in life, more deeply versed in prayer. But the priest has a special obligation to lead a devout life, to study divinity, to pray; and to be fit to give some help to his fellow-Christians in these supremely important concerns. Other people may expound the faith, and speak or write in Christ's name, more wisely and competently than the priest. They *may* do such things, and even do them better; the priest *must*: he must keep the congregation supplied with its staple diet: he must keep giving them some word from God ...

There is inevitably something absurd about our priesthood, because what we stand for is so infinitely greater than our poor little selves. But there's the same absurdity, really, about being a Christian at all. None of us can be let off being Christ in our place and in our station: we are all pigmies in giants' armour. We have to put up with it: it's the price (how small a price!) paid for the supreme mercy of God, that he does not wait for our dignity or our perfection, but just puts himself there in our midst; in this bread and in this wine: in this priest: in this Christian man, woman, or child.

He who gave himself first to us as an infant, crying in a cot, he who was hung naked on the wood, does not stand on his own dignity. If Jesus is willing to be in us, and to let us show him to the world, it's a small thing that we should endure being fools for Christ's sake, and be shown up by the part we have to play. We must put up with such humiliation of ourselves, or better still, forget ourselves altogether.

*A Celebration of Faith:* Austin Farrer

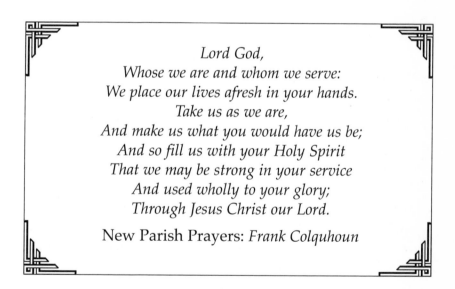

*Lord God,*
*Whose we are and whom we serve:*
*We place our lives afresh in your hands.*
*Take us as we are,*
*And make us what you would have us be;*
*And so fill us with your Holy Spirit*
*That we may be strong in your service*
*And used wholly to your glory;*
*Through Jesus Christ our Lord.*

New Parish Prayers: *Frank Colquhoun*

# Thursday after Lent 2: *Guarding your Tongue*

Donald Nicholl writes of his determination to control his tongue: "As the Buddhists teach, 'Learn, whenever you are on the point of speaking, to swallow your own words. If you can't swallow them, how can you expect others to do so?' Becoming holy is not all that complicated. All you have to do is what St James tells us: 'control our tongues', and then everything else in our life will fall into place." ... He attributes his silent attitude to a book entitled *Guard your Tongue,* a practical guide to avoiding derogatory speech based on the teachings of a Polish Rabbi, Chofetz Chayim. "Until I had studied Chofetz Chayim's compendium on the myriad ways in which one can sin through *leshon hora* (one's tongue of evil), I had never realized how much of our everyday conversation is corrupted through derogatory speech. Here one learns to appreciate the great strength of the rabbinic tradition, in that it does not allow one to escape into generalities but rather rubs one's nose in the concrete details of human behaviour. As, for example, if a person with whom you are conversing on the telephone insists on relating derogatory information, you should rebuke him even if the derogatory information is true. If this is not possible, you must find an excuse to hang up, saying 'Excuse me, something has just come up' (i.e. the derogatory information), and break off the conversation.

No wonder that some rabbis go so far as to say that tale-bearing is even more sinful than the cardinal sins of murder, adultery and idolatry. And no wonder it is a Jewish saint, James, who compares the evil tongue to the very tiniest spark which sets a huge stack of timber on fire, just as the tongue can send up a whole community in flames."

*The Testing of Hearts:* Donald Nicholl

*O Lord, give me a heart of compassion,*
*To put others' needs before my own.*
*Grant me the gift of humility, I pray,*
*That your grace may be sufficient for me.*

*For in my weakness, your strength is made perfect,*
*In my dependence, your glory is displayed.*
*May I receive your strength and wisdom,*
*Through your Spirit who dwells in me.*

*O Lord, I pray for love and understanding*
*For the suffering and hurt souls of this world,*
*That I may be your instrument of healing,*
*Your hands and feet and heart to serve.*

*May I bring lost souls to know you,*
*That they may feel your tender loving care,*
*As in your arms you enfold them,*
*Until in heaven your peace we share.*

The Times Book of Prayers

# Friday after Lent 2: *Come Home!*

To love is to give yourself away. You can dare throw yourself into the pilgrimage, because God has fallen in love with you so much that he has sent his son into the world to bring you home. This is the basic message of Christianity … Christianity is a love affair beginning with the gasp of astonishment with which all love affairs begin. Christianity is the School of Love. It is a hard school in which there are battles of life and death. It is the only school that matters.

Christianity, then, is an invitation to fall in love, an invitation to come home. It reminds me of the classic, if hackneyed, line in the play or the movie: "Come home, all is forgiven!" It is strange that our aching and our longing lead us away from the true object of our desire. Our longing has a double edge to it. It gives us an intimation of what we long for and yet shows us how far we have wandered from the path that leads to it. It is not unlike the experience of being on the "wrong" train or the "wrong" bus. We thought we knew where we were going, only we find that we're being taken further and further away from our desired destination. Dead ends serve a purpose. They bring us to ourselves … How, then, do we respond to our not being "at home"? Passion for pilgrimage leads us into the mystery of lostness from which we learn a new way of loving. This is what the season of Lent is all about. Its climax is Holy Week, which is the most solemn and momentous time in the Church's Year, when the love affair is revealed in all its wonder and glory. Its message is clear and simple: God has fallen in love with you and wants you to come home. We find ourselves in the middle of a love affair that is leading to a strange and terrible climax called the Crucifixion. We have an appointment with our Lover on Good Friday. It is a tryst we would rather not keep.

The kind of loving that leads to Good Friday seems crazy, foolish, and even irresponsible. Jesus turns my idea of loving upside down...

*Passion for Pilgrimage*: Alan Jones

*O Lord, into Thy hands I commend my spirit,*
*And the spirits of those whom I love.*
*Into Thy hands I commend the spirits of those who are*
*fearful,*
*Of death or life,*
*Of principalities and powers,*
*Of things present or of things that may never come.*
*Into Thy hands I commend the spirits of all those who*
*fear change,*
*More than they fear Thee,*
*Who put the law above justice, and order above love.*
*And help me this day to do some work of peace for Thee.*

Instrument of thy Peace: *Alan Paton*

# Saturday after Lent 2: *God Finding Me*

For most of my life I have struggled to find God, to know God, to love God. I have tried hard to follow the guidelines of the spiritual life – pray always, work for others, read the Scriptures – and to avoid the many temptations to dissipate myself. I have failed many times but always tried again, even when I was close to despair.

Now I wonder whether I have sufficiently realized that during all this time God has been trying to find me, to know me, and to love me. The question is not "How am I to find God?" but "How am I to let myself be found by him?" The question is not "How am I to know God?" but "How am I to let myself be known by God?" And, finally, the question is not "How am I to love God?" but "How am I to let myself be loved by God?" God is looking into the distance for me, trying to find me, and longing to bring me home. In all three parables which Jesus tells in response to the question of why he eats with sinners, he puts the emphasis on God's initiative. God is the shepherd who goes looking for his lost sheep. God is the woman who lights the lamp, sweeps out the house, and searches everywhere for her lost coin until she has found it. God is the father who watches and waits for his children, runs out to meet them, embraces them, pleads with them, begs and urges them to come home.

It might sound strange, but God wants to find me as much as, if not more than, I want to find God... I am beginning now to see how radically the character of my spiritual journey will change when I no longer think of God as hiding out and making it as difficult as possible for me to find him, but, instead, as the one who is looking for me while I am doing the hiding. When I look at my lost self and discover God's joy at my coming home, then my life may become less anguished and more trusting...

The parable of the prodigal son is a story that speaks about a love that existed before any rejection was possible and that will still be there after all rejections have taken place. It is the first and everlasting love of a God who is Father as well as Mother. It is the fountain of all true human love, even the most limited. Jesus' whole life and preaching had only one aim: to reveal this inexhaustible, unlimited motherly and fatherly love of his God and to show the way to let that love guide every part of our daily lives... It is the love that always welcomes home and always wants to celebrate.

*The Return of the Prodigal Son:* Henri J.M. Nouwen

*Lord, as I look at my hands,*
*I pray that they may stretch out to all who suffer,*
*That they may rest upon the shoulders of all who come*
*And that they may always offer the blessing*
*That emerges from the immensity of your love.*

# Lent 3: *Ministry and Spirituality*

Ministry and spirituality can never be separated. Ministry is not an eight-to-five job but primarily a way of life, which is for others to see and understand so that liberation can become a possibility.

There is today a great hunger for a new spirituality that is a new experience of God in our own lives. This experience is essential for every minister but cannot be found outside of the limits of his ministry. It must be possible to find the seeds of this new spirituality right in the centre of the Christian service. Prayer is not a preparation for work or an indispensable condition of effective ministry. Prayer is life; prayer and ministry are the same and can never be divorced. If they are, the minister becomes a handyman and the priesthood nothing more than another way to soften the many pains of daily life.

Jesus said: "A man can have no greater love than to lay down his life for his friends." For me these words summarize the meaning of all Christian ministry. If teaching, preaching, individual pastoral care, organizing, and celebrating are acts of service that go beyond the level of professional expertise, it is precisely because in these acts the minister is asked to lay down his life for his friends. There are many people who, through long training, have reached a high level of competence in terms of the understanding of human behaviour, but few are willing to lay down their own lives for others and make their weakness a source of creativity. For many individuals professional training means power. But the minister, who takes off his clothes to wash the feet of his friends, is powerless, and his training and formation are meant to enable him to face his own weakness without fear and make it available to others. It is exactly this creative weakness that gives the ministry momentum.

*Creative Ministry:* Henri J.M. Nouwen

*Father,*
*May your Holy Spirit kindle in our hearts a greater love*
*for Christ and his Church,*
*And make us fully alive to the opportunities of service*
*Which are ours in today's world.*
*Save us from complacency and fear of new ways;*
*Inspire us with a vision of a world won for you,*
*And stir our wills to pray and work and give*
*Until your will is done on earth as in heaven;*
*Through Jesus Christ our Lord.*

# Monday after Lent 3: *Being There*

"The newly ordained deacon was not sure what to expect as he called at the house. A short phone call from a friend of a young mother had only said that her child was ill and she needed someone from the church to come and talk. As he went in, he saw the four-year-old girl at play. She had a lump on her forehead, a tumour. Stripped so soon of the title and degree that had lengthened his name both ends, he was on the floor playing with balloons. Later when the girl became worse, he would be stripped further. All he could do was hold her when her mother could not be there. At the funeral he was stripped even more. There was nothing left and words could not fill the gap. His arms, like those of the mother's, were empty. All he could do was commend the girl into God's hands and arms. Theology was in being there, present and attentive, in the humility of bearing pain which must be contained in order to serve others and in order to reveal love" (Vanessa Herrick and Ivan Mann: *Jesus Wept: Reflections on Vulnerability in Leadership*).

"... the spirituality of those who care... is a spirituality of presence, of being alongside, watchful, available, of being there" (Sheila Cassidy: *Sharing the Darkness: The Spirituality of Caring*).

In both these examples of pastoral practice, theology is not something that falls neatly out of the skies, all pure and pearly-white, rather theological truth is in these contexts hard won: it emerges in the between-ness of persons who commit themselves to the often painful search for meaning and wholeness in the face of indefatigable heart-ache and sadness. Theology is about "staying with" when every nerve in the body screams, "walk away!"; theology is in the being, not in the saying, nor the doing, but in the stasis.

*"The Priest as Midwife: Towards a Theology of Pastoral Presence"*: Gareth Wynn Williams

Make me, O Lord, the instrument of thy love,
That I may bring comfort to those who sorrow
And joy to those who are regarded as persons of little account.
In this country of many races
Make me courteous to those who are humble
And understanding to those who are resentful.
Teach me what I should be to the arrogant and cruel,
For I do not know.
And as for me myself,
Make me more joyful than I am,
Especially if this is needed for the sake of others.
Let me remember my many experiences of joy and thankfulness,
Especially those that endure.
And may I today do some work of peace for thee.

Instrument of thy Peace: *Alan Paton*

# Tuesday after Lent 3: *A Learned Clergy*

I t is not given to every priest to be learned in the sense of amassing stores of factual knowledge, or of pursuing original research and investigation. He is not necessarily to be learned as the word is commonly used in secular usage. But he is called to be learned in the sense of being one who constantly wins fresh knowledge and fresh understanding of the faith which he teaches.

We teach, for instance, of God the Creator, of the Incarnation of the Son, of the mystery of the Cross, of the work of the Holy Spirit; and it matters greatly that our mind and imagination are, through constant searching and reflection, being quickened to freshness of grasp and wonder. In this sense there is no priest who cannot be learned and the promises in the ordination service pledge him so to be.

"Take heed to thy teaching." Make friends with the greatest writers, in biblical exposition, in Christian doctrine, in the classics of Christian spirituality.

Here is one rule within the reach of the busiest curate, and the busiest bishop: to make a special study of one book of the Bible every year.

*Durham Essays and Addresses:* Michael Ramsey

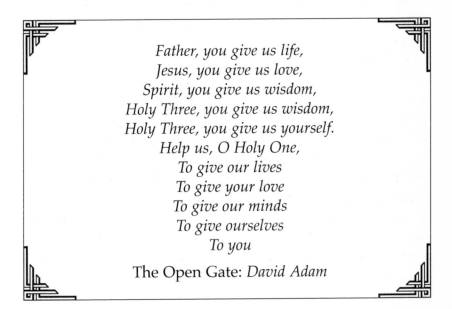

*Father, you give us life,*
*Jesus, you give us love,*
*Spirit, you give us wisdom,*
*Holy Three, you give us wisdom,*
*Holy Three, you give us yourself.*
*Help us, O Holy One,*
*To give our lives*
*To give your love*
*To give our minds*
*To give ourselves*
*To you*

The Open Gate: *David Adam*

# Wednesday after Lent 3: *True Forgiveness*

When the scarred and radiant Christ stood among his disciples on the evening of Easter Day, he was gathering into a community eleven men who were extremely frightened, confused and shocked. Their fellowship with Jesus during his mortal life had been the first essay in Christian community, and from the beginning it had been a failing community. Nearly every time its members opened their mouths they had revealed their inadequacies; but no failure had been like their last. In the days of Christ's Passover the community had disintegrated; when the Shepherd was struck the sheep were scattered. They were too terrified to stand by him, and during the next few days they were dragged through a series of shattering experiences: first shame and fear, then overwhelming grief and shock at his death, then emptiness and desolation, then bewilderment at confused tales from excited women of which they could make no sense. Then Jesus stood in their midst, saying, "Peace". No wonder they were dumbfounded.

He gathered them with no word of reproach, and gave them the peace purchased by suffering. They were forgiven, lifted into his joy, and sent to preach forgiveness of sins to all nations (cf. Luke 24:46-48). John makes it very explicit (see John 20:19-23).

Ever since that day, Christian community has been a place where people fail, and are seen to fail, and are forgiven. It has been a place where the risen Christ stands among us, bearing the wounds of our failures as transfigured scars, and breathing into us the Spirit of the new creation.

*Gateway to Hope:* Maria Boulding

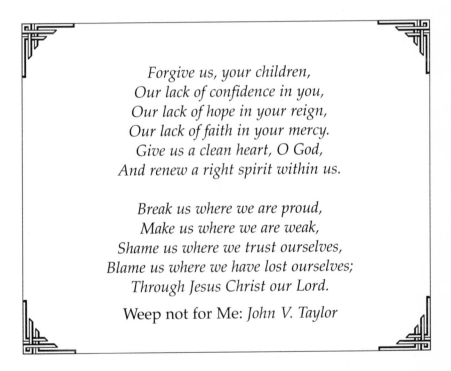

*Forgive us, your children,*
*Our lack of confidence in you,*
*Our lack of hope in your reign,*
*Our lack of faith in your mercy.*
*Give us a clean heart, O God,*
*And renew a right spirit within us.*

*Break us where we are proud,*
*Make us where we are weak,*
*Shame us where we trust ourselves,*
*Blame us where we have lost ourselves;*
*Through Jesus Christ our Lord.*

Weep not for Me: *John V. Taylor*

# Thursday after Lent 3: *"Come and Eat"*

J esus is always saying "Come and eat", whether it be to the crowd of 5000 in the desert, or to tax-collectors and sinners, or to the Twelve on the night before he died, or to two friends after the walk to Emmaus. It is always "Come and eat" and it is always bread that is on the menu.

In my own Christian pilgrimage, I have heard that invitation of Jesus more clearly than any other. Even when I have not been quite able to make out what following him might mean, even when I am somewhat resistant in taking up the cross or simply unable to fathom what is being asked of me, I have understood "Come and eat" and have responded. I have knelt, I guess, at a thousand different altars and at least half-heard the unchangeable words – "This is my body, this is my blood, do this in remembrance of me" – and stretched out my hands and taken what was offered and eaten it. Even when I have not been feeling very religious or prayerful, even when it has been difficult to concentrate on the words of the service because something else has been filling my mind, I keep hearing that invitation "Come and eat".

It is not always like that. Sometimes the worship is thrilling, the sense of God overwhelming, the experience of communion with him profound and real. Sometimes all distractions are banished. Christ is centre stage and I believe and trust, yearn and rejoice. But I do not believe that times like that are the only moments of grace. Mysteriously God can and does act when we are half-hearted, half-believing, half-uninterested, half-concentrating, providing we can produce just enough faith, staying power or openness to him to respond to that least complicated of invitations: "Come and eat".

But coming to eat is never an invitation to a comfortable supper party. Because of the fragmentation of the cross, there is cutting edge to this invitation...

*Signs of your Kingdom:* Michael Perham

*Lord, you have invited us*
*To be guests at your table.*
*You have welcomed us*
*Into your Presence.*
*You have fed us*
*with your body.*
*You have refreshed us*
*with your blood.*
*You have given us of your own self.*
*Help us to give ourselves to you,*
*In joy and thanksgiving,*
*In love and dedication.*
*As you give us freely,*
*Let us give freely to you.*

The Open Gate: *David Adam*

# Friday after Lent 3: *Christian Hope*

C. S. Lewis once wrote: "Hope is one of the theological virtues. This means that a continual looking forward to the eternal world is not (as some modern people think) a form of escapism or wishful thinking, but one of the things a Christian is meant to do. It does not mean that we are to leave the present world as it is. If you read history you will find that the Christians who did most for the present world were just those who thought most of the next. The Apostles themselves, who set on foot the conversion of the Roman Empire, the great men who built up the Middle Ages, the English Evangelicals who abolished the slave trade, all left their mark on Earth, precisely because their minds were occupied with Heaven. It is since Christians have largely ceased to think of the other world that they have become so ineffective in this. Aim at Heaven and you will get earth 'thrown in': aim at earth and you will get neither"…

More than ever today we need to hold fast our future hope… The call to discipleship is a call to God's promised glory. In view of the urgency of the times, we are to live lives that honour Christ, that heal wounds within his body, and that hasten the coming day of God. This is not a day in which to play religious games. Time is running out fast: Christ looks for disciples who are unashamed of him, bold in their witness, obedient to his word, united in his love and filled with his Spirit. There is no promise of an easy task. Joy and woe will be woven fine; tears, pain and sweat intermingled with radiant love and inexpressible joy. Christ wants disciples who will not only have hope, but will give hope. Whatever we receive we are to give away, that others too may rise through the darkness that covers the earth. "Arise, shine; for your light has come, and the glory of the Lord has risen upon you." Christ's disciples with such hope will change the course of this world.

*Discipleship:* David Watson

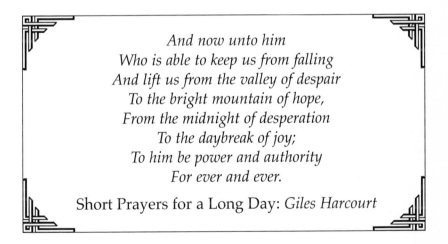

*And now unto him*
*Who is able to keep us from falling*
*And lift us from the valley of despair*
*To the bright mountain of hope,*
*From the midnight of desperation*
*To the daybreak of joy;*
*To him be power and authority*
*For ever and ever.*

Short Prayers for a Long Day: *Giles Harcourt*

# Saturday after Lent 3: *The Piercing Sword*

*T*he darkness is still with us, O Lord. You are still hidden and the world which you have made does not want to know you or receive you ... You are still obscured by the veils of this world's history, you are still destined not to be acknowledged in the scandal of your death on the cross ... But I, O hidden Lord of all things, boldly affirm my faith in you. In confessing you, I take my stand with you... If I make this avowal of faith, it must pierce the depths of my heart like a sword. I must bend my knee before you, saying, I must alter my life. I have still to become a Christian.

Karl Rahner: *Prayers for Meditation*

"The reading from Karl Rahner, at morning prayer, came as a shock. To hear so esteemed a theologian cry out, 'I have still to become a Christian' was humbling. The words have stayed with me all day. I wonder if one of the reasons I love the Benedictines so much is that they seldom make big noises about being Christians. Though they live with the Bible more intimately than most people, they don't thump on it, or with it, the way gorillas thump on their chests to remind anyone within earshot of who they are. Benedictines remind me more of the disciples of Jesus, who are revealed in the Gospel accounts as people who were not afraid to admit their doubts, their needs, their lack of faith. 'Lord, increase our faith,' they say. 'Teach us to pray.' They kept getting the theology wrong, and Jesus, more or less patiently, kept trying to set them straight.

Except for Peter, the disciples were not even certain who Jesus was: 'Have I been with you all the time, and still you do not know me?' Jesus asks in the Gospel of John, not long before he's arrested and sentenced to death.

" ... the image of the sword from Luke's gospel comes to mind as I walk back home after vespers (of the Feast of the Presentation). We've heard it twice today, at morning prayer and at Mass. I wonder if Mary is the mother of *lectio*, because as she pondered her life and the life of her son, she kept Simeon's hard prophecy in her heart ... Maybe Mary's story, and this feast, tell us that if the scriptures *don't* sometimes pierce us like a sword, we're not paying close enough attention."

*The Cloister Walk:* Kathleen Norris

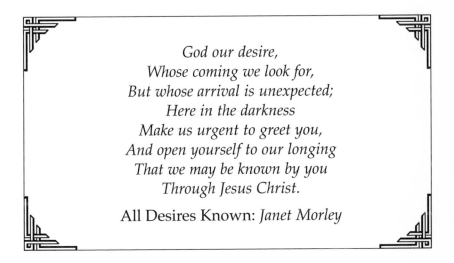

*God our desire,*
*Whose coming we look for,*
*But whose arrival is unexpected;*
*Here in the darkness*
*Make us urgent to greet you,*
*And open yourself to our longing*
*That we may be known by you*
*Through Jesus Christ.*

All Desires Known: *Janet Morley*

# Lent 4: *Transfiguration*

"He brought them up into a high mountain, apart by themselves, and he was transfigured before them." It did not mean that he had left behind him the conflicts of the Galilean ministry, which had gone before, or the conflicts of the *via crucis* which were to follow. That, perhaps, was St Peter's error, longing to linger in the glory of the mountain scene and to leave behind all that was irksome down below. Rather was it that, when our Lord went up to be transfigured, he carried with him every conflict, every burden, to be transfigured with him.

And when *we* go apart to be with Jesus in glory, it is so that our frustrations, our pains and our cares may be carried into that supernatural context which makes all the difference to them. These frustrations are not forgotten; they are not abolished; they can still be painful. But they become transfigured in the presence of Jesus, our crucified and gracious Lord.

And when we have carried our frustrations up to our Lord in his glory, we find in the days which follow that he generously brings his glory down right into the middle of our frustrations. "My peace I give unto you." "These things I have said unto you that my joy may be in you, and that your joy may be full." "Be of good cheer, I have overcome the world."

*Canterbury Essays and Addresses:* Michael Ramsey

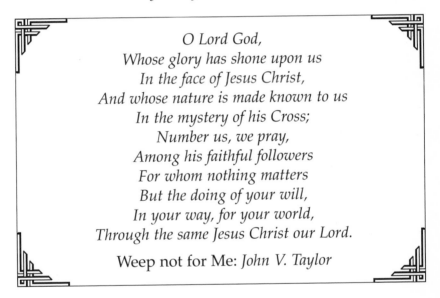

*O Lord God,*
*Whose glory has shone upon us*
*In the face of Jesus Christ,*
*And whose nature is made known to us*
*In the mystery of his Cross;*
*Number us, we pray,*
*Among his faithful followers*
*For whom nothing matters*
*But the doing of your will,*
*In your way, for your world,*
*Through the same Jesus Christ our Lord.*

Weep not for Me: *John V. Taylor*

# Monday after Lent 4: *Why Pray?*

...how necessary it is to view prayer as a discipline. Concentrated human effort is necessary because prayer is not our most natural response to the world. Left to our own impulses, we will always want to do something else before we pray. Often, what we want to do seems so unquestionably good – setting up a religious education programme, helping with a soup kitchen, listening to people's problems, visiting the sick, planning the liturgy, working with prisoners and mental patients – that it is hard to realize that even these things can be done with impatience and so become signs of our own needs rather than God's compassion. Therefore prayer is in many ways the criterion of Christian life. Prayer requires that we stand in God's presence with open hands, naked and vulnerable, proclaiming to ourselves and to others that without God we can do nothing. This is difficult in a climate where the predominant counsel is, "Do your best and God will do the rest." When life is divided into "our best" and "God's rest", we have turned prayer into a last resort to be used only when all our own resources are depleted... Discipleship does not mean to use God when we can no longer function ourselves. On the contrary, it means to recognize that we can do nothing at all, but that God can do everything through us. As disciples, we find not some, but all of our strength, hope, courage, confidence in God. Therefore, prayer must be our first concern.

*Compassion:* Nouwen, McNeil and Morrison

*Lord Jesus, you gave your life for me.*
*How can I respond to such love?*
*I give you my hands to do your work.*
*I give you my feet to go your way.*
*I give you my eyes to see as you do.*
*I give you my tongue to speak your words.*
*I give you my mind that you may think in me.*
*I give you my spirit that you may pray in me.*
*Above all, I give you my heart*
*that you may love in me your Father and all mankind.*
*I give you my whole self that you may grow in me*
*so that it is you, Lord Jesus,*
*who live and work and pray in me.*

# Tuesday after Lent 4: *Hidden in Christ*

J esus is hidden in our lives (as our lives are hidden in him, our deepest integrity and joy kept from our greedy eyes by being drowned in his glory), and so often hidden in our prayer. We would like our prayers to be conscious communion with Jesus or the Father; and time and again the experienced voices of Christian history tell us that this is not always or even often the norm. From time to time, we are, so to speak, allowed a short glimpse of what is really going on in us; but so fragile are these moments that we dare not quite rely on them and we cannot photograph them and pin them on the wall to reassure ourselves. But whether it is in the lonely dryness of a prayer that seems to be going nowhere or simply in the frustration of life that feels as if it is losing direction, God in Christ may be most fully alive. At least our own sense of doing well and satisfying expectations is not getting in the way. And we shall not know any of this while our journey continues, in ourselves or in anyone else. What this teaches us, though, is a proper reluctance to blot out or to try to forget any uncomfortable bits of our own lives, or to ignore or dismiss the Christian integrity of anyone else. Who knows where the life is coming through, where the well is rising?

People have often underlined the fact that prayer is less a matter of simply talking to Jesus than of letting Jesus talk to the Father in us. Sometimes it makes sense, certainly, to talk to Jesus, to turn to Jesus as saviour and friend in the most straightforward way; and he is there to hear. But the image of the Virgin of the Sign recalls us to what the friendship and saving work of Jesus is *for*: it is to bring us into the life that he lives and the prayer he prays. If that means, as it clearly does, that Jesus will not always be a distinct and comforting presence before our eyes, this is not a mark of spiritual failure; we are being taken gradually into the deep mysteriousness of his praying to the Father, a mysteriousness that we can only experience for a lot of the time as darkness and pathless desert. And when we find the hiddenness removed for some instant, it is not to reassure us that we have made a success of things, but to give us a hint of the wealth of Christ's life in us – a kind of momentary overhearing of the Word returning in power to the Father.

*Ponder these Things:* Rowan Williams

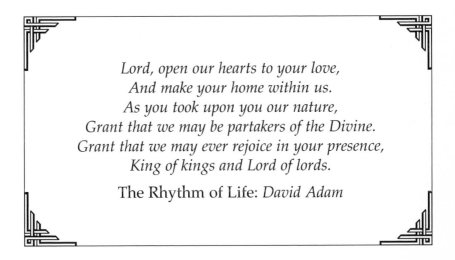

*Lord, open our hearts to your love,*
*And make your home within us.*
*As you took upon you our nature,*
*Grant that we may be partakers of the Divine.*
*Grant that we may ever rejoice in your presence,*
*King of kings and Lord of lords.*

The Rhythm of Life: *David Adam*

# Wednesday after Lent 4: *Called to Something Smaller*

We are not ordaining you to ministry; that happened at your baptism. We are not ordaining you to serve the Church in committees, activities, organisations; that is already implied in your membership.

We are not ordaining you to become involved in social issues, ecology, race, politics, revolution; for that is laid upon every Christian.

We are ordaining you to something smaller and less spectacular; to read and interpret those sacred stories of our community, so that they speak a word to people today; to remember and practise those rituals and rites of meaning that in their poetry address people at the level where change operates; to foster in community, through word and sacrament, that encounter with truth which will set men and women free to minister as the Body of Christ.

We are ordaining you to the ministry of the word and sacraments and pastoral care.

God grant you the grace not to betray but to uphold it, not to deny but affirm it, through Jesus Christ our Lord.

*Charge given at an Ordination Service in the Uniting Church in Australia in 1980*

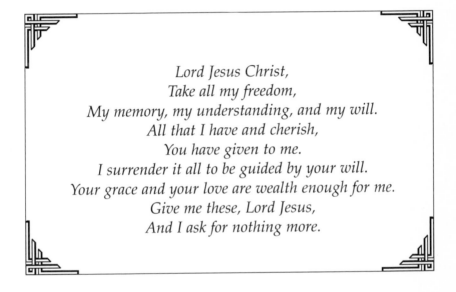

*Lord Jesus Christ,*
*Take all my freedom,*
*My memory, my understanding, and my will.*
*All that I have and cherish,*
*You have given to me.*
*I surrender it all to be guided by your will.*
*Your grace and your love are wealth enough for me.*
*Give me these, Lord Jesus,*
*And I ask for nothing more.*

# Thursday after Lent 4: *Sharing in the Journey*

The two travellers (journeying to Emmaus) had failed to believe in the resurrection, failed to find out more for themselves, failed to recognize Jesus and failed to understand the Scriptures, yet throughout their long walk the risen Christ was with them, sharing his Easter understanding with them, trying to open their bemused, frightened minds to the glory of his Easter, and theirs. "Don't you see...? Don't you remember that the Scriptures pointed to this? It is no accident; this is what they were trying to show: that God's Son, God's Christ, must suffer, and only through that gateway enter his glory. Let go of your plans, your hopes, your restricted, puny ideas. Your Father's love for you is greater than your hearts can conceive, because it is inseparable now from his love for me."

The identification holds. Christ's Passover to the Father is our Passover; Christ's long, dark journey is ours, and ours is his. He is in us and we are in him. In no part of the journey and in no place of failure are we ever alone. It is joyful because of him; there is great beauty along our road, and the certainty of his love. Prayer is our willing communion with a mystery of love far greater than our ideas or hopes or plans or vision, and as we fail bitterly in life and in prayer itself we are gently helped to bypass our limited expectations. Distress and bewilderment, knowing yet not knowing, the burning hearts, the realization afterwards that amid all the unknowing we did know, the closeness of Christ in word and sacrament: all this is an inspired picture of how things are, since Easter, along our road. He is more than a wayfarer with us; he is the Way.

Prayer is a long search, a dark journey; if we think of it as a journey to God we are not altogether wrong, but it is also a journey with God and a journey in God. He is not someone over against us, with whom we have to conduct a conversation or form a relationship. "In that day", said Jesus, the day which dawned at Easter and will see us into eternal life, "in that day you will know that I am in my Father, and you in me, and I in you" (John 14:20). There is nothing, "no-thing", between you and God.

*Gateway to Hope:* Maria Boulding

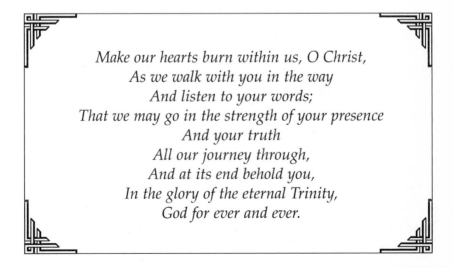

*Make our hearts burn within us, O Christ,*
*As we walk with you in the way*
*And listen to your words;*
*That we may go in the strength of your presence*
*And your truth*
*All our journey through,*
*And at its end behold you,*
*In the glory of the eternal Trinity,*
*God for ever and ever.*

# Friday after Lent 4: *Vocation*

Our Father in Heaven has called us each one to the place in which He can best satisfy His infinite desire to do us good. His inscrutable choice of the office or state of life or particular function to which we are called is not to be judged by the intrinsic merit of those offices and states but only by the hidden love of God. My vocation is the one I love, not because I think it is the best vocation in the Church, but because it is the one God has willed for me. If I had any evidence that He willed something else for me, I would turn to that on the instant. Meanwhile my vocation is at once my will and His. I did not enter it blindly. He chose it for me when His inscrutable knowledge of my choice moved me to choose for myself. I know this well enough when I reflect on the days when no choice could be made. I was unable to choose until His time had come. Since the choice has been made, there have been no signs in favour of changing it, and the presumption is that there will be no change. That does not mean there *cannot* be change.

If we are called to the place which God wills to do us the most good, it means we are called where we can best leave ourselves and find Him. The mercy of God demands to be known and recognized and set apart from everything else and praised and adored in joy. Every vocation is, therefore, at once a vocation to sacrifice and to joy. It is a call to the knowledge of God, to the recognition of God as our Father, to joy and understanding of His mercy. Our individual vocation is our opportunity to find that one place in which we can most perfectly receive the benefits of divine mercy, and know God's love for us, and reply to His love with our whole being.

That does not mean that our individual vocation selects for us a situation in which God will become visible to the eyes of our human nature and accessible to the feelings of our hearts of flesh. On the contrary, if we are called where we will find Him we must go where flesh and blood will lose Him, for flesh and blood cannot possess the Kingdom of God (I Corinthians 15:50). God sometimes gives Himself to us where He seems to be taken away.

*No Man is an Island:* Thomas Merton

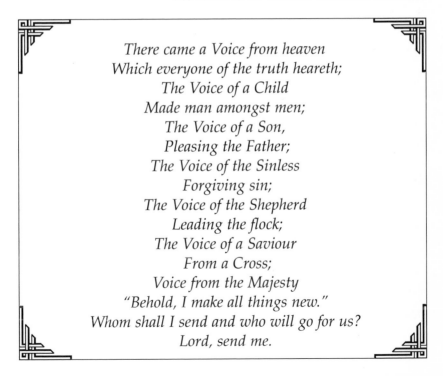

*There came a Voice from heaven*
*Which everyone of the truth heareth;*
*The Voice of a Child*
*Made man amongst men;*
*The Voice of a Son,*
*Pleasing the Father;*
*The Voice of the Sinless*
*Forgiving sin;*
*The Voice of the Shepherd*
*Leading the flock;*
*The Voice of a Saviour*
*From a Cross;*
*Voice from the Majesty*
*"Behold, I make all things new."*
*Whom shall I send and who will go for us?*
*Lord, send me.*

# Saturday after Lent 4: *Reading the Bible around Jesus*

We need to read the Bible, as is often said, around Christ, and read it, therefore, in the confidence that our own mishearing and misapprehending, our own confusions and uncertainties about the text and about the matter with which it deals, are going to be part of God's triumphant work in us...

Now reading the Bible around Jesus, with all that in mind, is by no means easy and, as we know all too well, in the Church it can lead to endless squabbles and bitterness. We do not know how to read certain passages: we do not know how to deal properly with Paul in his most rampantly masculine moods; we do not know how to deal with some texts on sexuality; we do not know how to cope with the violence of so much of Hebrew scripture. We may say the psalms each day and quite often find ourselves wishing unspeakable plagues on our enemies. All the time we need to remember what kind of humanity it is in which, to which and through which God speaks: a broken humanity, a humanity badly equipped to receive God's liberty. Yet we can recognise this not simply with resignation or cynicism. We do not read the Bible just as a record of the crimes and follies of mankind, to paraphrase Gibbon in *The Decline and*

*Fall of the Roman Empire,* but as a record of how those crimes and follies are drawn together and plaited into a strong rope, drawn together and unified in the Word made flesh. As the text of encounter and contest is fulfilled in our own struggles, so we pray that the culmination of that text, the Word Incarnate, may triumph in each one of us, in our reading, in our praying and in our living.

*Open to Judgement:* Rowan Williams

*Lord God, our Father,*
*open our eyes to what you wish to reveal to us.*
*Give us understanding of the sacrifice you ask of us,*
*and the courage and faith to accept your will;*
*for the love of your Son, Jesus Christ our Lord.*

With Christ in the Wilderness:
*Derek Worlock and David Sheppard*

# Lent 5: *Being Vulnerable*

T he road through the wilderness has led us to the foot of the cross. We have gone through the untried and the unknown only to find ourselves at "the place of the skull," a crucible of transformation. We would rather not go on. We would rather be enslaved by an unthinking certainty, and there is plenty of the trashy and tinselly kind of religion to give us what we want.

Think about your basic needs… We long to have someone keep our conscience so that we are relieved of the responsibility of having to think things through. The temptation is to imagine that we can ever get to a place where we don't have to struggle anymore with the ambiguities and uncertainties of life. Our longing for miracle, authority, and mystery was prefigured in the temptations of Jesus in the wilderness. He turned his back on them and made his way to Jerusalem. We must do the same. Our longing for miracle, authority and mystery can easily be exploited by those who peddle magic, tyranny and mystification. Think of your own temptation to be enslaved by what you perceive to be your needs. Think how open you are to the tyranny of some form of mystification.

Think about your *God-given* vulnerability. It is a gift! It makes you available to God and to others. All our adventures on the Pilgrim's Way have been to help us see the gift in our vulnerability. We live in the faith of God's love and not in the "certainty" of our own position. We can now catch a glimpse of the fact that there may well be a kind of certainty from which we would like to be saved. There is the kind of certainty that kills the passion of the heart. It would have us all marching the goose-step down the great road of life, in serried ranks, all cloned from a "true believer," all with the same fixed smile. But that isn't what we are about. The freedom won on the cross brings with it both doubt and responsibility. That is why we dread it.There is no way around the Passion… to be a child of God is to know the meaning of suffering and delight. To be a child of God is to enter the mystery of the Passion and become a divine experiment in vulnerability. Our pain is the pain of new life seeking to burst out in us – a life that embraces everyone. We have come a long way toward finding our true home. We get that much closer when we face the dread that the promise of freedom and faith brings. We get closer when we accept ourselves as experiments in vulnerability. We get even closer when we are able to receive the healing words, *Come home. All is forgiven!*

*Passion for Pilgrimage:* Alan Jones

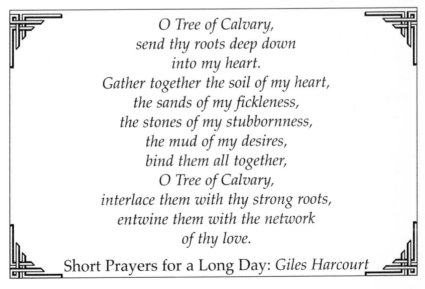

*O Tree of Calvary,*
*send thy roots deep down*
*into my heart.*
*Gather together the soil of my heart,*
*the sands of my fickleness,*
*the stones of my stubbornness,*
*the mud of my desires,*
*bind them all together,*
*O Tree of Calvary,*
*interlace them with thy strong roots,*
*entwine them with the network*
*of thy love.*
Short Prayers for a Long Day: *Giles Harcourt*

# Monday after Lent 5: *The Celtic Way*

The Celtic tradition reminds us that asceticism is a profound means of spiritual growth. Consideration of this may well make us ask if it is possible to recover any meaningful asceticism today in a culture of affluence, of instant satisfaction, consumerism, self-fulfilment. Yet there are already many signs that the world wants to draw back. This does not of course refer to those who have no such choice, the hungry for whom the possibility of voluntary fasting is non-existent, but to the average, comfortable middle-class person who is beginning to find that they are looking for restraint at many levels. This may be a more simple life-style, the training and subduing of the body, whether by jogging, dieting, health farms, or whatever the current enthusiasm is, and in particular addressing the conquering of those addictions which hold the body in thrall. Limitation, asceticism, restraint, discipline here have no end: the escape from tyranny and the movement towards freedom, so that destructive forces may be replaced by life-giving forces. Perhaps the Celtic tradition will help with the rediscovery of the role of asceticism in religious practice in its widest sense, not only at the level of fasting and penance, but by an affirming and unspectacular acceptance of the place of discipline, restraint, simplicity in daily life. The importance of the soul-friend, a spiritual guide who will help the individual to find their own path (for he or she is, in the phrase used by the seventeenth century Benedictine Augustine Baker, "only God's usher") is becoming more and more commonly recognized. The way of sorrow and repentance and reparation is not to be taken alone. Here is support so that the journey back to God, this *metanoia* of turning and returning, becomes the way to freedom and fullness of life.

*Celtic Light:* Esther de Waal

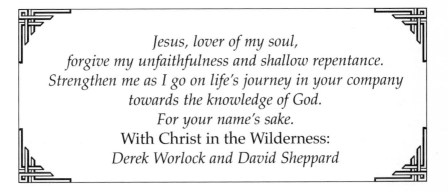

*Jesus, lover of my soul,*
*forgive my unfaithfulness and shallow repentance.*
*Strengthen me as I go on life's journey in your company*
*towards the knowledge of God.*
*For your name's sake.*
With Christ in the Wilderness:
*Derek Worlock and David Sheppard*

# Tuesday after Lent 5: *To be Born is to be Chosen*

For millions of years, before you arrived here, the dream of your individuality was carefully prepared. You were sent to shape the destiny in which you would be able to express the special gift you bring to the world. Sometimes this gift may involve suffering and pain that can neither be accounted for nor explained. There is a unique destiny for each person. Each one of us has something to do here that can be done by no-one else. If someone else could fulfil your destiny, then they would be in your place, and you would not be here. It is in the depths of your life that you will discover the invisible necessity which has brought you here. When you begin to decipher this, your gift and giftedness come alive. Your heart quickens and the urgency of living rekindles your creativity.

If you can awaken this sense of destiny, you come into rhythm with your life. You fall out of rhythm when you renege on your potential and talent, when you settle for the mediocre as a refuge from the call. When you lose rhythm your life becomes wearingly deliberate or anonymously automatic. Rhythm is the secret key to balance and belonging. This will not collapse into false contentment or passivity. It is the rhythm of a dynamic equilibrium, a readiness of spirit, a poise which is not self-centred. This sense of rhythm is ancient. All life came out of the ocean; each one of us comes out of the waters of the womb; the ebb and flow of the tides is alive in the ebb and flow of our breathing. When you are in rhythm with your nature nothing destructive can touch you. Providence is at one with you; it minds you and brings you to your new horizons. To be spiritual is to be in rhythm.

*Anam Cara:* John O'Donohue

*From the flowing of the tide*
*To its ebbing*
*From the waxing of life*
*To its waning*
*Of your Peace provide us*
*Of your Goodness give us*
*Of your Grace grant us*
*Of your Power protect us*
*Of your Love lift us*
*And in your Arms accept us*
*From the ebbing of the tide*
*To its flowing*
*From the waning of life to its waxing.*

Tides and Seasons: *David Adam*

# Wednesday after Lent 5: *The Fire and the Clay*

The priestly life is public and it is sacramental. It is another particularizing, as both encouragement and witness. In specific acts of service it may rightly be said that effectiveness and validity do not depend on the worthiness or faith of the priest. The heart of the priest's ministry is the making visible of the gift of personhood which is Christ's alone. It is no accident that the parish priest in England became known as the *persona* who represents Christ to his people. Such representation demands an integrity of faith and life that both points to Christ and reveals the fruitfulness of faith in Christ. It demands that the priest be one who has an evident confidence in Christ as the giver of the self.

Much of our human experience is of disappointment and failure. We long to "be someone" yet our hopes seem unattainable. In response, the Christian tradition reveals to us the God who creates and redeems. What seemed futile and empty is set before us afresh in terms of offer and gift. George Herbert, in a poem called simply "Priesthood", takes two powerful and ancient images. He speaks of us as clay, and God, the maker and redeemer, as fire. At once we see the distance from God that talk about sin indicates and we sense the power of God to overcome the gap. Jesus Christ is the giver of God; and the Christian priest, through a life of faith in the giver and service to the Church which is his body, is called to be a gift to the world – to open the eyes of the blind and bring liberty to the captives – so that the clay of the world may be transformed by the fire of God. If we are to appreciate the distinctiveness of the priest's calling we must give our attention to the shape of the Church, for only within and as a part of the Church does any talk of a priest make sense.

*The Fire and the Clay:* Peter Allan

*Grant, O Lord,*
*that the same mind be in all of us*
*that was in Christ Jesus:*
*his self-forgetting humility,*
*interest in common things,*
*his love for common people,*
*compassion for the fallen,*
*his tolerance with the mistaken,*
*his patience with the slow,*
*and in our work make us continually*
*sensitive to your guidance*
*and ready for your will,*
*through Jesus Christ our Lord.*

Short Prayers for a Long Day: *Giles Harcourt*

# Thursday after Lent 5: *Renewed for Service*

It is through these fragile, frail, and earthen vessels that we exercise the ministry entrusted to us by Christ in his Church, a ministry of so great excellency yet of so great difficulty. John Sanford, in his book *Ministry Burnout*, touches very appropriately on the nature of the ministerial task – the repetitive aspect of much of our work, not least the way we prepare for and conduct the liturgy and worship of the Church; the constant demands made upon us from so wide a variety of people, the impossible expectations of so many; our involvement with education, with homelessness, with drugs, with alcohol and a good deal else besides, as we attempt to ensure the Church, in the place where it is set, responds as best it can practically and effectively in Christian love and service. Then there are the urgent and unexpected things which cut into and cut across the best laid plan... Such demands, such pressures, such expectations, can lead in all of us to some degree of tension between what I might call the inwardness and the outwardness which arises from the fact of any public ministry. It is something we have to live with all the time, even in the more domestic matter of fact things; for instance, inside you are feeling lousy, ground down, spiritually at a low ebb, not quite up to it, and yet you still have to go into the school to do the assembly, say nice things to the Mothers' Union and woo the choir into singing something more appropriate for the bishop's visit than three anthems in succession. So how do you cope? How do we survive this impossible and crazy business called Christian Ministry, the pattern for which is given us so eloquently in the Lord's washing of the disciples' feet?

I dare to venture that in spite of all we may say, teach or preach, all of us are to a very large extent caught up in "self-justifying works", so that "amazing grace" is almost a stranger to us. Yet it is in and through "amazing grace" that the Lord has laid his hands upon us, to call us out into a ministry in his Church, and to authorise and empower that ministry entrusted to us. Furthermore it is only in and through amazing grace that our ministry is nurtured, encouraged and enabled, and ourselves built up into a holy temple to the Lord. There is, therefore, an urgent need in our Church for the renewal of our lives in the power of the Holy Spirit, not least those of us who do exercise a distinctive ministry. We need to reflect deeply and carefully upon what has been laid upon us, so that there shall indeed be a real harmony and consonance between the inwardness and the outwardness of our calling; a harmony and coherence, though, which is only possible to the extent to which we are prepared not to be conformed to the things of this world but rather to allow the transforming power of the Holy Spirit to be at work in every part of us – the dark side just as much as the bright side; in every aspect of our lives so that we may prove what the will of God is, what is good, acceptable and perfect.

*Living the Gospel:* David Hope

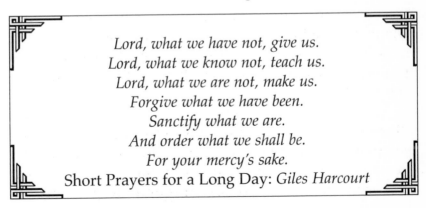

*Lord, what we have not, give us.*
*Lord, what we know not, teach us.*
*Lord, what we are not, make us.*
*Forgive what we have been.*
*Sanctify what we are.*
*And order what we shall be.*
*For your mercy's sake.*
Short Prayers for a Long Day: *Giles Harcourt*

# Friday after Lent 5: *True Reconciliation*

In my own experience the receiving and acceptance of God's forgiveness produces in me a sense of reconciliation with God that inspires in me a willingness to offer forgiveness to others. Indeed, it produces in me a determination to seek reconciliation with my enemies at whatever cost. The cost is sometimes considerable. It may mean risking snubs, rejection, cruel words, deliberate attempts to reduce me to a condition of near slavery as a price to be paid for that reconciliation. Those attempts have to be resisted, because the only kind of reconciliation worth having is that which is made from a position of freedom shown by Christ when he went to the cross. Yet, if I can retain that sense of acting from a place of freedom, I can sense sometimes, perhaps not very often, but certainly sometimes, that the Holy Spirit is acting to free the other person, or group of people, from their need to oppress and subject and destroy. Then they can receive my forgiveness and return it. Truly, one can then return thanks to God.

The choice to forgive, to say "enough is enough", can liberate people from being chained to the past, from being distorted persons, from being unable to move on to freedom. Once they realize this, they can make a deliberate choice to forgive...

I think that the greatest gift I have received from my long experience of a personal struggle to forgive, and through accompanying other people on their journeys through pain to forgiveness, sometimes through forgiveness to reconciliation, has been that of a grateful heart. There is, of course, much pain and disappointment in this kind of work, much distress for all concerned when marriages break down, for instance, or when parents and children are irreconcilable, or when people have to leave employment because of injustice, or when communities of people cannot learn to live together in harmony. That disappointment is balanced by gratitude for the courage of so many people who come sick and leave well, even if that has also meant the irretrievable breakdown of a cherished relationship. Above all, my grateful heart has come from being allowed the privilege of seeing God's reconciling person of Christ at work in my own and so many other people's lives.

*Forgive and Live:* Una Kroll

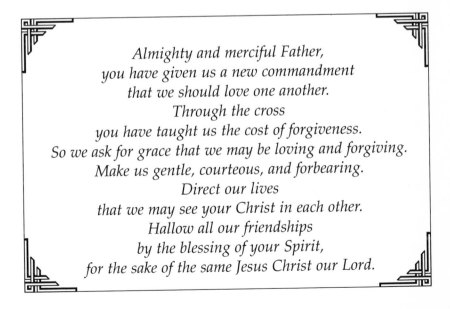

*Almighty and merciful Father,*
*you have given us a new commandment*
*that we should love one another.*
*Through the cross*
*you have taught us the cost of forgiveness.*
*So we ask for grace that we may be loving and forgiving.*
*Make us gentle, courteous, and forbearing.*
*Direct our lives*
*that we may see your Christ in each other.*
*Hallow all our friendships*
*by the blessing of your Spirit,*
*for the sake of the same Jesus Christ our Lord.*

# Saturday after Lent 5:
## *Knowing Christ in our Hearts*

Paul prayed that Christ might dwell within the hearts of his readers (Ephesians 3:17). To know Christ is to know his presence in our hearts. I vividly remember a conversation some years ago with Donald Coggan, a former archbishop of Canterbury. We were discussing some of the challenges to theological education, and had ended up by sharing our concerns over people who left theological education knowing a lot more about God but seemingly loving God rather less than when they came in. Coggan turned to me sadly and remarked: "The journey from head to heart is one of the longest and most difficult that we know." I have often reflected on that comment, which I suspect reflects his lifelong interest in theological education and the considerable frustrations it generated – not to mention his experiences of burnt-out clergy, who seemed to have exhausted their often slender resources of spiritual energy and ended up by becoming a burden instead of a gift to the people of God.

A head-knowledge of God may well be better than no knowledge of God at all. But it leaves a lot to be desired... It is not enough to know God by description; we must know him within the intimacy of a relationship. It is perfectly possible to know about Christ without having encountered him as a living and life-changing reality. *We can easily assent to the truth of the gospel, yet find something else more attractive and meaningful.* Our mind may assent to the truth of Christ, but our hearts find their consolation through someone or something else. Our hearts must recognise Christ as the fulfilment of all their secret desires and longings before we can truly know him.

*Knowing Christ:* Alister McGrath

*Lord Jesus our Saviour*
*Let us now come to you:*
*Our hearts are cold;*
*Lord, warm them by your selfless love.*
*Our hearts are sinful;*
*Cleanse them with your precious blood.*
*Our hearts are weak;*
*Strengthen them with your joyous Spirit.*
*Our hearts are empty;*
*Fill them with your divine presence.*

*Lord, our hearts are yours;*
*Possess them always*
*And only for*
*YOURSELF.*

# Passion Sunday (Palm Sunday):
## *The Way of the Cross*

Innumerable crowds of people have lovingly, obediently, walked in the footsteps of Christ, treading the long way, the tragic way which is shown by our Lord, a way tragic but which leads from this earth to the very throne of God, into the Kingdom of God. They walk, carrying their crosses, they walk now for two thousand years, those who believe in Christ. They walk on, following him, crowd after crowd, and on the way we see crosses, innumerable crosses, on which are crucified the disciples of Christ. Crosses, one cross after the other, and however far we look, it is crosses and crosses again. We see the bodies of the martyrs, we see the heroes of the spirit, we see monks and nuns, we see priests and pastors, but many, many more people do we see, ordinary, simple, humble people of God who have willingly taken upon themselves the cross of Christ. There is no end to this procession. They walk throughout the centuries knowing that Christ has foretold us that they will have sorrow on this earth, but that the Kingdom of God is theirs. They walk with the heavy cross, rejected, hated, because of truth, because of the name of Christ. They walk, they walk, these poor victims of God, the old and the young, children and grown-ups. But *where are we?* Are we going to stand and look; to see this long procession, this throng of people with shining eyes, with hope unquenched, with unfaltering love, with incredible joy in their hearts, pass us by? Shall we not join them, this eternally moving crowd, that is marked as a crowd of victims, but also as little children of the Kingdom? Are we not going to take up our cross and follow Christ? Christ has commanded us to follow him. He has invited us to the banquet of his Kingdom and he is at the head of the procession. Nay, he is together with each of those who walk. Is this a nightmare? How can blood and flesh endure this tragedy, the sight of all these martyrs, new and old? Because Christ is Risen, because we do not see in the Lord who walks ahead of us the defeated prophet of Galilee as he was seen by his tormentors, his persecutors. We know him now in the glory of the Resurrection. We know that every word of his is true. We know that the Kingdom of God is ours if we simply follow him.

*Meditations on a Theme:* Anthony Bloom

*O Lord, our Saviour and God,*
*Whom nails could not hold to the Cross, but only love:*
*Grant that we,*
*Who have received the fullness of thy love,*
*May be ready to bear before the world the marks of thy*
*Passion;*
*Who livest and reignest with the Father and the Holy*
*Spirit, one God,*
*World without end.*

Procession of Passion Prayers: *Eric Milner-White*

# Monday in Holy Week: *The Road to Love*

Holy Week is a time for our hearts to burst, a time to trust our own inner experiences of things, which tells us that in the breaking of the heart there is new life, new power, new energy. But I have no stomach for the cost. The gateway to life and the road to love is through God's Passion. No wonder we resist it. No wonder we domesticate the cross and try to trivialize its impact. Yet I continue to be fascinated by the love revealed here. I am drawn to it even as I am repelled by it. There is a kind of passion – even a  kind of pain – for which we are starved. Unless we get back in touch with the passion and the pain, we are already as good as dead. The reason is simple. God is at the heart of this passion and pain, and where God is there is life in all its fullness. That is why all but the hardest of hearts are moved by the Passion Story. It strikes chords deep within us and plays a music too deep for words.

Anthony Bloom, the Russian Orthodox archbishop in London, once observed, "Of course the Christian God exists. He is so absurd, no one could have invented him!" There is an important truth here. If you were to invent a God, you could do a lot better than the broken God of Calvary. Jesus reveals a God who is a victim. What kind of a God is that? In Jesus, we see a God who is vulnerable, a God who betrays himself into our hands. God is at our mercy. What is the use of a God like that? To add insult to injury, the Christian tradition claims that we are made in the image of this weak and vulnerable deity!

You belong to this God. Many a time you have fancied a deity of your own devising. You have even thought of yourself in the role of God. Well, now is your chance. Your moment is coming. If you want to know what God is like, look at Jesus. If you want to be like God, be like Jesus.

*Passion for Pilgrimage:* Alan Jones

*O Lord Jesus Christ,*
*whose Cross hath painted bright thy love:*
*Imprint on our hearts the love with which*
*thou hast loved us;*
*that we may display thy likeness along all our paths,*
*unto all for whom thou hast died;*
*who livest and reignest in the glory of the eternal Trinity,*
*God for ever and ever.*

Procession of Passion Prayers: *Eric Milner-White*

# Tuesday in Holy Week: *Involved in the Passion*

The Cross of Jesus Christ cannot be observed objectively from a position of detachment. To be there at all is to be involved, implicated one way or another. That is why all but one of the disciples was not there: they were not ready to be involved. The daughters of Jerusalem were not ready to be involved, they preferred to pity. Pity is one of the most deceptive of human emotions. It is a half-way stopping place on the way to discipleship. Yet at no time did Jesus ask us to pity him, or to pity his brothers and sisters in whom we are meant to find him.

We are called to feed them and clothe them, visit them in sickness and in prison. We are called to become involved in them at the level of our wills and our action. So if we are to pay attention to his passion and resurrection this week we shall become involved somehow or other. Our whole existence may become involved, since there is no part of it which is untouched by this event.

But we shall not really become involved in the Passion of Jesus unless we also are willing to be involved more deeply in our world. And when I say "more deeply", I mean we must learn to see the sufferings of the hungry and oppressed and powerless in the light of this crucifixion. For that is the true mystery of the Cross. Here every human suffering and every human evil is focused into one single event – the dying of the Son of God. As the light and warmth of the sun spread across the landscape is concentrated through a lens to produce one point of intense heat, so in the Cross of Jesus we see all the wrong and injustice of the long human story, all the agonies and griefs of the human race, focused in upon this one sufferer: the Lamb of God who carries the sin of the world. Here is the meaning of it all. Here is the truth of it all. Here is the way through it all and the promise of ultimate salvation...

The true perspective of our lives is not the small, moderate bourgeois world that we pretend is ours but a cosmic stage on which the great extremes of the Gospel are stark realities – light and darkness, life and death, luxury and starvation, heaven and perdition. In this struggle of immense opposites the Cross of Jesus Christ towers to its true height. For in the world as it is today nothing can avail to save us but an act of God making available once more to humanity the divine wisdom and strength and love.

*Weep not for Me:* John V. Taylor

*Saviour of the world,*
*we marvel at the salvation you have accomplished:*
*help us to walk with you in the way of the cross,*
*together with your other children,*
*and to discover your victory*
*through failure and pain.*
*We make this prayer*
*that our Father's name may be glorified.*

With Christ in the Wilderness:
*Derek Worlock and David Sheppard*

# Wednesday in Holy Week: *The Cross in L'Arche*

As they were crowding around the cross and kissing the feet and head of Jesus, I closed my eyes and could see his sacred body stretched out and crucified upon our planet earth. I saw the immense suffering of humanity during the centuries: people killing each other; people dying from starvation and epidemics; people driven from their homes; people sleeping on the streets of large cities; people clinging to each other in desperation; people flagellated, tortured, burned, and mutilated; people alone in locked flats, in prison dungeons, in labour camps; people craving a gentle word, a friendly letter, a consoling embrace, people – children, teenagers, adults, middle aged, and elderly – all crying out with an anguished voice: "My God, my God, why have you forsaken us?"

Imagining the naked, lacerated body of Christ stretched out over our globe, I was filled with horror. But as I opened my eyes I saw Jacques who bears the marks of suffering in his face, kiss the body with passion and tears in his eyes. I saw Ivan carried on Michael's back. I saw Edith coming in her wheelchair. As they came – walking or limping, seeing or blind, hearing or deaf – I saw the endless procession of humanity gathering around the sacred body of Jesus, covering it with their tears and their kisses, and slowly moving away from it comforted and consoled by such great love. There were sighs of relief; there were smiles breaking through tear-filled eyes; there were hands in hands and arms in arms. With my mind's eye I saw the huge crowds of isolated, agonizing individuals walking away from the cross together, bound by the love they had seen with their own eyes and touched with their own lips. The cross of horror became the cross of hope, the tortured body became the body that gives new life; the gaping wounds became the source of forgiveness, healing, and reconciliation. Père Thomas and Père Gilbert were still holding the cross. The last people came, knelt, and kissed the body, and left. It was quiet, very quiet.

Père Gilbert then gave me a large chalice with the consecrated bread and pointed to the crowd standing around the altar.

I took the chalice and moved among those whom I had seen coming to the cross; looked at their hungry eyes and said, "The body of Christ... the body of Christ... the body of Christ" countless times. The small community became all humanity, and I knew that all I needed to say my whole life was, "Take and eat. This is the body of Christ."

*The Road to Daybreak:* Henri Nouwen

*Jesus, may all that is in you flow into me.*
*May your body and blood be my food and drink.*
*May your passion and death be my strength and life.*
*Jesus, with you at my side enough has been given.*
*May the shelter I seek be the shadow of your cross.*
*Let me not run from the love which you offer.*
*But hold me safe from the forces of evil.*
*On each of my dyings shed your life and your love.*
*Keep calling me until the day comes,*
*When, with the saints*
*I may praise you for ever.*

# Maundy Thursday: *The Eucharistic Life*

What is meant by the "eucharistic life"? It doesn't mean going to church every five minutes, and it doesn't mean walling oneself in with Christian thoughts and Christian friends, important though these are. Rather, it means reproducing in everyday life the pattern of the Eucharist, which is the pattern of Christ: living a life to which penitence and forgiveness are integral; open to the glory of God in even the most unexpected settings; listening for his Word in whatever is said, and in the spaces between; testing one's belief against the belief and unbelief of the world; offering oneself for others, and others to God; entering into the darkness, brokenness and bloodiness of things in the nakedness of unprotected faith; and enjoying to the full our communion, our community with people of every possible kind, and with the whole created order. We pray God to make us a living sacrifice, but by itself that's too narrow and negative: we must become, in fact, a living *sacrament*, giving with love and receiving with thanks.

Such a life could not be artificially engineered ("now how am I going to integrate penitence into my meeting with Ken this morning?...and did I really rejoice in my communion with Auntie's poodle last Monday?"); and it could never be more than partially realized. But it *will* be partly realized if we let the words and actions of the Eucharist sink into our souls; and through that regular and costly prayer which keeps our life open to the dimension of God and the reality of his Kingdom, and imperceptibly converts our whole life into an act of prayer and praise. Our real response to the Word of the Lord, and to the gift of his Body and Blood, is not a piously muttered (or earnestly shouted) formula: our true Amen, beginning from that moment, is the life we live.

*Bread of the World:* John Hadley

*Lord,*
*as you agonize and pray this night,*
*forgive us our weary neglect*
*of all those in need*
*whose wants we do not recognize.*
*Give us watchful eyes*
*to discover the beauty of your face,*
*hidden beneath the world's sorrow.*
*Help us to be the hands of your compassion*
*and a sign of your love.*
*Through the same Jesus Christ our Lord.*

With Christ in the Wilderness:
*Derek Worlock and David Sheppard*

# Good Friday: *Love to the Loveless*

...If I can now forgive, it is only because I have been forgiven, I and all other men and women who have ever lived. Certainly one can forgive only what has been done to oneself. But all the evil ever done has been done to God, because it is a misuse of his good gifts, a rejection of the purposes he set in motion from the beginning. The crucified Jesus is the only accurate picture of God the world has ever seen, and the hands that hold us in existence are pierced with unimaginable nails. But on this Cross God fulfils the nature of forgiveness by using the evil done to him as the means of a new good; for it is the Cross of Jesus which creates within me a free, unhesitating acceptance of the law of love...

Jesus is the image and likeness of God in human terms; he has done God's work in human space and time. Faced with this truth, I cannot stop there. I have to go beyond it to an even greater affirmation, because of the very nature of love. It is inconceivable to me that love should ever say: "I must save these children of mine, and that will mean the most terrible suffering. *I will find someone else to do the job.*" Love does not send others to suffer in its place. Love comes itself. And at this point I am struck dumb. I dare not frame the thought that faces me, and yet there is no other thought to which I can turn and escape. This is no clever theory, no remote possibility, no wild imagination. It is something that I *know*. It is absurd, it cannot possibly be true, but deep inside there is no question about it. The Cross is not a picture of God. This was God himself.

...When God, who is just such love through and through, enters a particular world, he can do so only in a form which will allow that love full play; and in our case that means the form of a Man. This then is the family likeness between God and ourselves; not our brains, not our self-awareness, not our conscience – just our love.

*The Foolishness of God:* J. Austin Baker

*Lord Jesus Christ,*
*lifted up that all may see what it is to love:*
*Grant us so to behold and be drawn to that love,*
*that with our whole strength*
*we may love you and all for whom you died,*
*who now lives and reigns in the unity of*
*the Father and the Holy Spirit, God, for ever and ever.*

Procession of Passion Prayers: *Eric Milner-White*

# Easter Eve: *Victory!*

...for many centuries the men and women of our land visualised the cross not primarily as the instrument of suffering and death, but as the symbol of victory and life. Dr Michael Ramsey in his book *The Resurrection of Christ,* rightly draws attention to this misplaced tendency in Christian thought and devotion in the past to concentrate on the sufferings of Christ on the cross, and to overlook the aspect of victory.

It was Bishop Westcott who, in one of his *Village Sermons* preached in the early years of this century wrote:

"If our eyes have been holden hitherto, they need to be holden now no longer. Christ is waiting as at this time to reveal his passion and his victory. He holds out to us his cross, the symbol not of suffering only, but of triumph. Let us look to that, and we shall find in it all wisdom and hope. As we strive to work for God, times of doubt and difficulty, of mistrust and discouragement, must come. It may seem, when we have done it all, that the realm of darkness is still unenlightened, the power of evil still unchecked. But let us be of good cheer. Christ reigns from the cross."

"Christus vincit, Christus regnat, Christus imperat": "Christ conquers, Christ reigns, Christ rules". Those who have ever joined with other Christians in this great shout will know the thrill that it brings, and the consciousness of being fellow-sharers with him in his victory...Our life would be without purpose or meaning were our devotion to end at the cross. If the poet Venantius Fortunatus, to whom we owe so much, could set down those Passiontide hymns, "The royal banners forward go", and "Sing, my tongue, the glorious battle", he could also write the glorious processional hymn for Easter morning:

"Hail thee, Festival day! Blest day that art hallowed for ever;
Day wherein Christ arose, breaking the kingdom of death".

The cross, then, is not the end of the story. An unknown Englishman, writing towards the close of the fourteenth century, concludes what is described as one of the most devout of all Passion prayers with the words which each one of us in this century may repeat as his or her own prayer:

*Jesus make me then to rise*
*From death to life, on such a wise*
*As thou rose up on Easter Day,*
*In joy and bliss to live for aye. Amen.*

*The Cross in English Life and Devotion:* Gordon Huelin

# Easter Day: *Alive for Ever and Ever!*

Today is one of the most glorious muddles in the whole of the New Testament. You'd have thought that accounts of this day of all days would have tallied! All the Gospel writers have a different tale, a different emphasis. There are stones rolling back and no stone, there is one angel and two, several different women who either do or do not pass on the good news and a whole lot of disciples who either believe or not!

Surely it would have made sense to stick to one storyline, God? But what it shows is that everyone wanted to be part of it and I'm sure everyone knew someone who had been there when – and this is the wonderful truth shared by all of them – when Jesus came back to life. But you know, when we consider this glorious truth, we must see it in its full context. Mary Magdalene will have her special memories – and I so love Jesus for singling out one of his favourite cracked pots for special attention. Peter and John will have their own stories. Even the Roman soldiers had a tale to tell.

But we are the most fortunate because we have all the accounts. We have the hindsight memories of Peter at the time of Pentecost – and we have the amazing revelation of John that the Jesus who came back is in fact the risen Lord in all his glory.

I turned round to see the voice that was speaking to me. And when I turned I saw seven golden lampstands, and among the lampstands was someone "like a son of man", dressed in a robe reaching down to his feet and with a golden sash round his chest. His head and hair were white like wool, as white as snow, and his eyes were like a blazing fire. His feet were like bronze glowing in a furnace, and his voice was like the sound of rushing waters. In his right hand he held seven stars, and out of his mouth came a sharp double-edged sword. His face was like the sun shining in all its brilliance.

When I saw him, I fell at his feet as though dead. Then he placed his right hand on me and said: "Do not be afraid. I am the First and the Last. I am the Living One; I was dead, and behold I am alive for ever and ever! And I hold the keys of death and Hades."

(Revelation 1:12-18, NIV)

And to me this is the best truth of all. All-mighty, all-powerful, it is he who stands and knocks at the door of our hearts. He who wants to come into the house of our life and eat with us and we with him. The risen Lord of Glory whose face shines like the sun. The Holy One of God, our creator and our dearest friend.

*The Apple of his Eye:* Bridget Plass

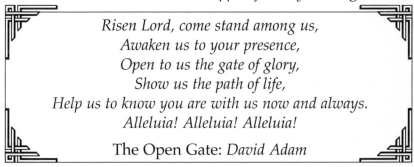

> *Risen Lord, come stand among us,*
> *Awaken us to your presence,*
> *Open to us the gate of glory,*
> *Show us the path of life,*
> *Help us to know you are with us now and always.*
> *Alleluia! Alleluia! Alleluia!*
>
> The Open Gate: *David Adam*

**The compiler is grateful to the following for permission to reproduce copyright material for this book:**

Bible Reading Fellowship:
*The Apple of his Eye* by Bridget Plass (1996).

Bishop David Sheppard (Bible Reading Fellowship):
*With Christ in the Wilderness* by David Sheppard and Derek Worlock (1990).

Church in Wales Publications:
*Theology Wales* (Winter 1999), "The Priest as Midwife: Towards a Theology of Pastoral Presence" by Gareth Wynn Williams.

Continuum:
*Forgive and Live* by Una Kroll (2000).
*Meditations on a Theme* by Anthony Bloom (1974).
*Signs of Hope* by David Hope (2001).

Darton, Longman & Todd:
*Bread of the World* by John Hadley (1989).
*Compassion* by Henri Nouwen et al. (1982).
*Here and Now* by Henri Nouwen (1994).
*The Joy of the Saints* ed. Robert Llewelyn (1988).
*Living the Gospel* by David Hope (1993).
*Open to Judgement* by Rowan Williams (1994).
*The Return of the Prodigal Son* by Henri Nouwen (1994).
*Road to Daybreak* by Henri Nouwen (1988).
*Taste and See* by Margaret Silf (1999).
*The Testing of Hearts* by Donald Nicholl (1989).

Doubleday:
*Creative Ministry* by Henri Nouwen (1991).

Margaret Duggan (ed.):
*Through the Year with Michael Ramsey* (Hodder & Stoughton, 1975).

Friends of York Minster:
*A Procession of Passion Prayers* by Eric Milner-White (reprinted 1962).

Ruth Gledhill (ed.):
*The Times Book of Prayers* (Mowbray, 1997).

Harper Collins:
*Celtic Light* by Esther de Waal (1997).
*Gateway to Hope* by Maria Boulding (1985).
*Short Prayers for a Long Day* compiled by Giles and Melville Harcourt (1978).

Hodder & Stoughton Ltd:
*I Believe in the Church* by David Watson (1978).
*A Celebration of Faith* by Austin Farrer (1970).
*New Parish Prayers* by Frank Colquhoun (1982).

Dean Alan Jones (Grace Cathedral, San Francisco):
*Passion for Pilgrimage* (HarperSanFrancisco, 1989).

Lion—Hudson plc:
*The Cloister Walk* by Kathleen Norris (1996).

Rev. Professor Alister E. McGrath:
*Knowing Christ* (Hodder & Stoughton, 2001).

Morehouse Publishing (USA rights):
*The Open Gate* by David Adam (1994).
*The Rhythm of Life* by David Adam (1996).

Janet Morley:
*All Desires Known* (originally published by the Movement for the Ordination of Women, 1988).

Random House Ltd:
*Anam Cara* by John O'Donohue (1999).

St Paul's:
*To be a Pilgrim* by Basil Hume (1984).

SCM Press:
*Letters and Papers from Prison* by Dietrich Bonhoeffer (enlarged edn, 1971).

SCM—Canterbury Press:
*Ponder these Things* by Rowan Williams (2002).

Simon & Schuster Inc. (USA rights):
*Letters and Papers from Prison* by Dietrich Bonhoeffer (enlarged edn, 1971; reprinted with permission: Scribner, an imprint of Simon & Schuster Adult Publishing Group © 1953, 1967, 1971 by SCM Press Ltd).

SPCK:
*The Fire and the Clay* by George Guiver et al. (1999).
*The Open Gate* by David Adam (1994).
*The Rhythm of Life* by David Adam (1996).
*Signs of your Kingdom* by Michael Perham (2002).
*Tides and Seasons* by David Adam (1989).

The Tablet Publishing (www.thetablet.co.uk):
*In Good Company: The Fast Track from the Corporate World to Poverty, Chastity and Obedience* by James Martin SJ.
*A Sermon at Greenbelt* by Tony Campolo.

William Neill-Hall Ltd (Literary Agency):
*Discipleship* by David Watson (Hodder Paperback edn, 1973).
*Through the Year with Michael Ramsey* ed. Margaret Duggan (Hodder, 1975).